BULLETPROOF
DIET
SMOOTHIE:

A Beginner's Guide to the Bulletproof Diet: Recipes to help you Lose up to 1LBS Every Day, Regain Energy and Live a Healthy Lifestyle.

By
Dave Scott

Copyright © 2019 by: Dave Scott

ISBN-13: 978-1-950772-38-4
ISBN-10: 1-950772-38-1

All Rights Reserved. No part of this publication may be reproduced in any form or by any means, including scanning, photocopying, or otherwise without prior written permission of the copyright holder.

Disclaimer:

The information provided in this book is designed to provide helpful information on the subjects discussed. The publisher and author are not responsible for any specific health or allergy needs that may require medical supervision and are not liable for any damages or negative consequences from any treatment, action, application or preparation, to any person reading or following the information in this book.

Table of Contents

INTRODUCTION 6
  STICK TO THE BULLETPROOF DIET 6
BULLETPROOF SMOOTHIE YOUR DIET TO LOSING WEIGHT, UPGRADE YOUR LIFESTYLE AND END FOOD CRAVINGS FOR GOOD 8
  Avocado Shake Recipe: 8
  Avocado-Banana Smoothie 9
  Avocado Milkshake 10
  Avocado Shake or Smoothie 11
  Chocolate!! Avocado Paleo Smoothie Recipe 12
  Avocado Chocolate Peanut Butter Smoothie 13
  Chocolate Avocado Strawberry Smoothie Recipe 14
  Avocado Berry Banana Breakfast Smoothie 15
  Avocado Mango Smoothie 16
  Avocado, Mango, and Pineapple Smoothie 17
  Avocado Mango Lime Smoothie Recipe 18
  Mango Banana Avocado Smoothie with Chia Seeds 19
  Banana Orange Smoothie 20
  Breakfast in a Cup 21
  Caramelized Tropical Peach Smoothie 22
  Cashew Coconut Creamer (Dairy free) 23
  Chocolate Coconut Banana Protein Shake 24
  Chocolate Coconut Smoothie 25
  Coconut Blueberry Smoothie 26
  Coconut Cream Mocha 27
  Coconut Date Shake 28
  Coconut Eggnog Smoothie 29

- Coconut Fruit Smoothie 30
- Coconut Latté 31
- Coconut Peanut Butter Banana Protein Shake 32
- Coconut Pumpkin Pie Smoothie 33
- Coconut Smoothie 34
- Coconut Tropical Bliss Smoothie 35
- Coconutty Green Smoothie 36
- Creamy Coconut Cinnamon Smoothie 37
- Dark Chocolate Raspberry Custard Smoothie 38
- Energy Berry Smoothie 39
- Fresh Fruity Smoothie with Coconut Oil 40
- Fruit-Coconut Smoothie 41
- Fruity Tropical Smoothie 42
- Get Your Greens Smoothie 43
- Hot Cocoa 44
- Iced Coconut Mocha Cappuccino 45
- Hot Fudge Sauce 46
- Non-Dairy Coconut-Mocha Coffee Creamer 47
- Pecan Coconut Chocolate Milk 48
- Carrot Coconut Candy 49
- Post-Holiday Power Smoothie 50
- Quick Tropical Coconut Smoothie 51
- Raspberries & Cream Breakfast Smoothie 52
- Raspberry Coconut Smoothie 53
- Raspberry Peach Melba Smoothie 54
- Rise & Shine Breakfast Smoothie 55
- Sensational Banana Strawberry Smoothie 56
- Strawberries & Coconut Cream Protein Shake 57
- Strawberry Coconut Bliss Smoothie 58

BULLETPROOF DIET SMOOTHIE

Strawberry Lemon Coconut Smoothie 59
Strawberry Mango Coconut Delight 60
Strawberry Vanilla Coconut Smoothie 61
Tropical Cocktail 62
CILANTRO WITH SPINACH SMOOTHIE 63
KIWI AND APPLE GREEN SMOOTHIE 64
COCONUT, APPLE AND YOGURT GREEN SMOOTHIE 65
CHOCOLATE COVERED CHERRY GREEN SMOOTHIES 66
RAW CHOCOLATE ALMOND GREEN SMOOTHIE 67
AVOCADO GREEN SMOOTHIE 68
DATES AND CASHEWS GREEN SMOOTHIE 69

INTRODUCTION

STICK TO THE BULLETPROOF DIET

Ask yourself the number of times you started out on a new diet with the greatest of intentions of getting healthier and losing weight only for everything to fall apart faster than you can say.

Dave Asprey in the bulletproof diet cookbook turned conventional diet wisdom on its head, outlining the plan responsible for his 100-pound weight loss, which he came to by "biohacking" his body and optimizing every aspect of his health. He urges for one to gain energy, build lean muscle, and watch the pounds melt off (just as he and so many of his devoted followers already have) you have to stop counting calories, eat high levels of healthy saturated fat, skip breakfast, work out less, sleep better, and add smart supplements.

The Bulletproof Diet could be called an "upgraded" Paleo diet. The condition is simple all you do is to eat a high (healthy!)-fat, low carb diet, getting 50-60% of calories from healthy fats, 20% from protein, and the remaining from vegetables. A major disagreement between Bulletproof and Paleo is the ability to minimize toxins from the diet which are thought to play a major role in inflammation.

The bulletproof diet marked a significant moment in my approach to nutrition and health, and changed a lot of things in my life. You should understand that when it comes to losing weight, your diet is much more important than your exercise habits (for instance, losing weight is maybe 80% diet and 20% exercise). You can exercise all you want but if you're not taking care of your diet you are going to find it very difficult to strip off excess body fat.

I have been everywhere from intense neurofeedback centers to Tibetan monasteries. My experience in the bulletproof diet is unique, which is one of the major reasons for this book.

The main reasons Paleo works well is because it removes grains from the diet, which are a very high source of mold contamination. Getting toxins out of your diet can effectively help you reduce inflammation and lose weight, even if you are not particularly sensitive.
This book is a great sit-down read, as well as a beginner's guide to the bulletproof diet.

This book contains other "hacks" as described in the Bulletproof Diet, which will make you feel really transform. I personally assure you that you will feel your best (sharper, happier, calmer) eating the high fat diet that Dave recommends in his book. I have recommended this type of diet to my clients and many have testified that the feel calmer, happier and have lost weight, without feeling hungry or unsatisfied.

However, if you have ever battled with weight issues, energy levels, focus throughout the day, mood swings, or any other nagging issues that you think might be holding you back, I highly recommend this book to you, and check out Even if you aren't actively working on fixing one of those troubles, you owe it to yourself to try this stuff.
In addition, bulletproof Diet lets you experiment and change it up so that it works for you and your preferences. You do not have to count calories or measure your food. Instead, foods are arranged in a handy spectrum so you can choose in respect to how bulletproof you want to become.

To crown everything up, the diet recommends 60% of your diet should be "healthy" fat, 20% good quality meat, and the rest vegetables and a tiny bit of starch and It also promotes taking supplements. Have it in mind that there is No calorie counting, eat when hungry and stop when you're full and also No snacking between meals, and kick off the day with a bulletproof coffee.

BULLETPROOF SMOOTHIE YOUR DIET TO LOSING WEIGHT, UPGRADE YOUR LIFESTYLE AND END FOOD CRAVINGS FOR GOOD

Avocado Shake Recipe:

Ingredients:
2 cups of ice (about 16 to 20 ice cubes)
½ to 1 cup of cold non-fat milk
1 ripe avocado (peeled and pitted)
½ cup of fat-free sweetened condensed milk

NOTE: Remember that the best avocados to use are those that gently yield to pressure and are free from dark blotches inside the fruit. In the other hand, it depends on how large the avocado is and how thick you want your shake.

Preparation:
1. First, you scoop the avocado flesh into a blender.
2. After which you add the ice cubes, condensed milk, the least amount of non-fat milk; puree until completely smooth.
3. Then you taste and add additional milk if a thinner consistency is desired (NOTE: I prefer using the maximum amount of milk.)
4. Finally, you pour into two (2) tall glasses and enjoy!

Avocado-Banana Smoothie

Ingredients
2 banana
3 cups of fresh orange juice (from 6 oranges)
5 to 6 cups ice
 2 avocado
1 cup of nonfat plain Greek yogurt
½ cup of honey

Directions
1. First, you combine avocado, banana, honey, yogurt, orange juice, and ice in a blender.
2. After which you blend until smooth.
3. Then you serve immediately.

Avocado Milkshake

Ingredients
2 (28 ounces) evaporated milk
6 cups of ice cubes
8 avocados
1 cup of sugar
2 teaspoons of lemon juice

Directions:
1. First with a knife, halve avocados and remove pit.
2. After which you use a spoon, scoop flesh and cut into cubes.
3. After that, combine avocados, milk, sugar, lemon juice and ice in a blender.
4. Then you process until smooth and blended.

Avocado Shake or Smoothie

Ingredients

4 cups of crushed ice
Honey, Agave or Sugar (6-8 tablespoons if using brown sugar), to taste
4 Avocados (preferably ripe)
2 cups of milk, plus more if needed (for Paleo sub with Almond or better still Coconut Milk)

Procedure

1. First, you place the crushed ice in a blender.
2. After which you top it with the avocado.
3. After that, you add the rest of the ingredients.
4. Then you process until smooth and thick to your desired consistency.
5. Feel free to add more milk if you want just an easy pour kind of shake (I prefer mine a little thick and creamy).
6. However, if you are feeling rather indulgent, I suggest you add some whipped cream and garnish it with a cherry on top!

Chocolate!! Avocado Paleo Smoothie Recipe

Ingredients
4 frozen bananas
4 cups of almond or better still coconut milk
2 avocados
1 cup of frozen raspberries (or better still fresh raspberries or other berries)
2-4 tablespoons of unsweetened cocoa powder

Directions:
NOTE: If you have unpeeled frozen bananas, then you should take the frozen bananas from the freezer and leave to thaw for 10 minutes before peeling (or better still cut the skin off with a paring knife).
1. First, you place all the ingredients into a blender and blend well.
2. Enjoy!

Avocado Chocolate Peanut Butter Smoothie

Ingredients
2 mediums ripe frozen banana
6 tablespoons of creamy peanut butter
1 teaspoon of vanilla extract (optional, but recommended)
1 medium avocado
4 tablespoons of cocoa powder
3 cups of unsweetened vanilla almond milk (preferably more or less to desired consistency)
2 tablespoons of agave nectar, zero-calorie sweetener, or honey (more or less to taste)

Directions:
1. First, you add everything into a blender and blend on high for about 2 - 4 minutes, or until smooth and creamy.
2. Then you add more milk as necessary to reach your desired thickness.
3. Enjoy!

BULLETPROOF DIET SMOOTHIE

Chocolate Avocado Strawberry Smoothie Recipe

Ingredients
2 ripe avocado (roughly chopped)
3 cups of almond or better still coconut milk
Dark chocolate, grated (it is optional)
2 cups of frozen strawberries
2 tablespoons of cocoa powder
1 teaspoon of vanilla
2 tablespoons of raw honey (it is optional)

Directions:
1. First, you place all the ingredients in a blender, and pulse until everything is smooth.
2. Then pour mix into 2 large glasses, and sprinkle grated dark chocolate on top.

Avocado Berry Banana Breakfast Smoothie

Ingredients
1 ripe frozen banana
1 cup of frozen berries
4 cups of spinach, romaine (or better still other dark leafy green)
1 ripe avocado
2 cups of nut milk or water
2/3 cup of oats

Optional: 1 or 2 Medjool dates, pitted

Directions:
1. First, you scoop the avocado flesh out of its skin, discarding the pit.
2. After which you place everything into a blender and blend until smooth and creamy.
3. Enjoy!

Notes: make sure you choose all organic ingredients if possible

Avocado Mango Smoothie

Ingredients:
1 pitted avocado
2 cups of almond milk (regular milk or coconut milk also works great)
2 cups of frozen mango
1 cup of Greek Yogurt
2-4 Tablespoons of honey

Optional add-in: 2-4 drops Orange essential oil
Directions:
First, you place all ingredients in a blender and blend until smooth.

Avocado, Mango, and Pineapple Smoothie

Ingredients
2 ripe medium avocados, pitted, peeled and diced (about 2 cups)
1 cup of diced pineapple (about 6 ounces)
2 tablespoons of agave nectar
1 cup of unsweetened coconut water
3 cups of diced mango (about 18 ounces)
10 ice cubes

Directions:

1. First, you add coconut water, avocado, mango, pineapple, ice, and agave nectar to blender.
2. After which you blend on high about 30 seconds until completely smooth.
3. Then you divide between two glasses and serve immediately.

Avocado Mango Lime Smoothie Recipe

Ingredients
½ avocado (peeled and seed removed)
2-4 ice cubes (it is optional)
A cup of filtered or better still spring water
½ cup of fresh (or better still frozen mango chunks)
Juice of ½ a lime

The Add-ons
½ teaspoon of ginger spice
1 tablespoon of coconut oil
½ fresh or better still frozen banana

Directions:
First, you place all of the ingredients into your blender and blend for 30-45 seconds or until the desired consistency is reached.

BULLETPROOF DIET SMOOTHIE

Mango Banana Avocado Smoothie with Chia Seeds

Ingredients
2 banana (frozen)
1 cup of Greek yogurt
Sweetener to taste (I prefer 2 tablespoons of honey)
2 cups of mango (from 2 small Ataulfo mango)
1 avocado
1 cup milk (preferably any kind you prefer)
2 tablespoons of chia seeds

Directions:
1. First, you blend all ingredients together in a food processor or blender until combined and smooth.
2. After which you add more milk for thinner consistency.
3. Then you serve immediately since avocado tends to turn brown after a while.

Banana Orange Smoothie

Ingredients:
1 cup of orange juice (more or less, depending on how thick or thin you want it)
2 tablespoons of Concentrate Coconut Cream
6 ice cubes
2 banana
6 tablespoons of virgin coconut oil, liquefied
6 tablespoons of organic whole milk vanilla yogurt

Directions:
1. First, you put the entire ingredient in a blender and blend until it is well incorporated.

2. If you wish, feel free to add 10 frozen strawberries.

BULLETPROOF DIET SMOOTHIE

Breakfast in a Cup

Ingredients:
1cup of rolled oat flakes
1 cup of coconut peanut butter (or peanut butter)
Dash cinnamon
2 cups of spinach (it is optional)
4 frozen bananas
2 cups of milk (feel free to use more or less to adjust to desired consistency)
2-4 tablespoons of coconut oil, melted
2 teaspoons of vanilla

Directions:
1. First, you place the entire ingredients in a good blender and blend until it is smooth and well mixed.

2. After which you pour into glasses and serve immediately.

Caramelized Tropical Peach Smoothie

Ingredients:
8 soy-free egg yolks (it is optional, but feel free to add lots of sustaining nutrition and energy)
4 tablespoons of coconut flakes
1 ¼ cups of frozen peaches
Dash salt
3 cups of coconut milk (plain kefir or grass-fed milk)
2 tablespoons of virgin coconut oil, melted
2 tablespoons of whole sugar (+/- to taste – remember that this is what gives it the delicious, caramelized flavor)
2 teaspoons of vanilla extract
1 cup of frozen pineapple

Directions:
1. First, you blend the entire ingredients thoroughly until smooth.

2. After which you stir in a small amount more whole sugar to each serving for a delicious caramel crunch, i.e. if you wish.

BULLETPROOF DIET SMOOTHIE

Cashew Coconut Creamer (Dairy free)

Ingredients:
½ cup of honey
4 tablespoons of coconut oil, melted (give or take as needed)
2 cups of cashew nuts (soaked overnight, rinsed)
1 teaspoon of vanilla extract
1 cup of coconut milk

Directions:
1. First, you place the entire ingredients in high-powered blender.

2. After which you blend until smooth and creamy, pouring melted coconut oil in to the mix in a steady drizzle.

3. Then you store in glass jar in the refrigerator for up to a week.

BULLETPROOF DIET SMOOTHIE

Chocolate Coconut Banana Protein Shake

Ingredients:
2 teaspoons of cocoa
½ teaspoon of guar gum (it is optional)
1 ¼ cups of water
2-6 tablespoons of coconut oil (melted)
2-4 heaping scoops of double bonded chocolate protein powder
½ teaspoon of xanthan gum (it is optional)
2 frozen bananas
1 cup of coconut milk (or organic raw whole milk)
10 ice cubes, it is optional (more or less as needed)

Directions:
1. First, you add the entire ingredients except coconut oil to blender and blend, pouring the coconut oil in slowly.

2. Then continue blending until smooth.

Chocolate Coconut Smoothie

Ingredients:
4 tablespoons of organic golden flax seeds
2 teaspoons of organic cocoa powder
2 teaspoons of organic vanilla extract, (opt)
2 chopped pear
Ice cubes, as required
Approximately 1 ¼ cup of dates or raisins soaked in 2 cups of water
2 tablespoons of shredded (or flaked coconut)
2 - 4 teaspoons of coconut oil
2 teaspoons of organic whole sugar (or to taste)
2-4 frozen chopped bananas

Directions:
1. First, you soak the date/raisin, shredded or flaked coconut and organic golden flax seeds from 30 minutes to a couple of hours.

2. After which you blend slowly in a blender and then add other ingredients and then blend well.

3. Feel free to top this with raw cacao nibs or add other seeds/nuts as desired.

Coconut Blueberry Smoothie

Ingredients:
1 cup of organic blueberries
4 tablespoons of organic whole milk plain yogurt
12-16 ice cubes (depending on your preferred quantity)
12 oz. organic coconut milk
1 banana
2 tablespoons of virgin coconut oil

Directions:
1. First, you toss the entire ingredients in the blender and blend well until frothy.

2. Then you pour into a glass and serve.

Coconut Cream Mocha

Ingredients:
2/3 cup of sugar or honey
1 cup of water
3 - 4 cups of strong black coffee
Ice cream, of your choice for garnish (it is optional)
1 cup of cocoa powder
7 cups of whole milk
½ cup of coconut cream concentrates
4 teaspoons of vanilla extract
Whipped cream, for garnish (it is optional)

Directions:
1. First, you stir together cocoa and sweetener, in a large saucepan with a wire whisk.

2. After which you add 2 cup of milk, the water and coconut cream concentrate, over medium heat.

3. After that, you whisk and bring to a simmer.

4. At this point, you add coffee and the remaining milk and whisk until mocha is nice and hot.

5. Finally, you add vanilla.

   7. Feel free to remove from heat and serve with a spoonful of the optional garnishes if you wish.

Coconut Date Shake

Ingredients:
4 tablespoons of Coconut Cream Concentrate (or preferable more to taste)
4 cups of ice (more or less depending on the desired thickness)
28 oz. of coconut milk
Small handful of dates (pits removed, more or less to taste)
4 teaspoons of coconut oil, melted
1 cup soaked almonds or Brazil nuts for extra protein (Soak for at least an hour and rinse off water).

Directions:
1. First, you place the entire ingredients in the blender.

2. While you are still blending, pour the coconut oil into the shake in a slowly.

3. Then blend all really well for a great, healthy, non-dairy desert or breakfast drink.

Coconut Eggnog Smoothie

Ingredients:

10 large soy-free eggs
4 tablespoons of coconut cream concentrate (softened)
1 teaspoon of ground ginger
8-10 frozen ripe bananas
3 cups of raw milk (or coconut milk)
4 tablespoons of virgin coconut oil (melted)
1 teaspoon of nutmeg
1 teaspoon of cinnamon
½ teaspoon of sea salt

Directions:

1. First, you blend the entire ingredient except the bananas until thoroughly mixed.

2. After which you add the frozen bananas and blend until smooth.

3. Make sure you serve immediately with an extra sprinkle of nutmeg on top.

BULLETPROOF DIET SMOOTHIE

Coconut Fruit Smoothie

Ingredients:
1-2 whole bananas
4 tablespoons of fresh ground flax seeds
2 tablespoons of coconut oil (melted)
2 cups of coconut milk (or regular whole milk)
4 tablespoons of fresh groundnuts (such as almonds, pecans, etc.)
½ cup of frozen fruit (such as berries, peaches, etc.)
2 tablespoons of dry coconut (such as flakes, etc.)

Directions:
1. First, you place the entire ingredients except coconut oil in blender and blend.

2. After which you slowly pour coconut oil into blender while blending.

3. Then you blend until smooth and then serve.

BULLETPROOF DIET SMOOTHIE

Coconut Latté

Ingredients:
2-6 tablespoons of coconut oil
4 tablespoons of coconut flavored syrup (or preferred flavor and amount)
2-4 tablespoons of coconut cream concentrate (it is optional)
1 ¼ cups of whole milk
2 cups of espresso

Directions:
1. First, you brew espresso and add flavored sweetener of your choice (or omit) and coconut cream concentrate if you using it.

2. After which you pour into serving mugs.

3. Then you use espresso steamer, to steam milk and coconut oil to 140 degrees.

4. Finally, add to espresso and serve.

BULLETPROOF DIET SMOOTHIE

Coconut Peanut Butter Banana Protein Shake

Ingredients:
2 frozen bananas
2/3 cup of coconut milk
Dash guar gum (it is optional)
2-4 tablespoons of melted coconut oil (suitable for pre-workout)
2 serving vanilla protein powder
1 ¼ cups of water
2-4 tablespoons of Coconut Peanut Butter
Dash xanthan gum (it is optional)
Ice to taste (it is optional)

Directions:
1. First, you place the entire ingredients except coconut oil (if using) in blender and blend while you pouring coconut oil in a steady stream.

2. Then you blend until smooth and then serve.

Coconut Pumpkin Pie Smoothie

Ingredients:
2 bananas (fresh or frozen)
2 dashes of cinnamon
2 tablespoons of coconut oil (melted)
½ cup of pumpkin puree
1 cup of coconut milk
2 teaspoons of honey

Directions:
1. First, you combine pumpkin puree, banana, coconut milk, cinnamon, and honey in a blender.

2. After which you blend on high until well mixed and smooth.

3. Then while the blender is still running, you slowly pour in the coconut oil.

4. Finally, you pour in a glass and garnish with a sprinkle of cinnamon.

5. Enjoy!

Coconut Smoothie

Ingredients:
2 cups of water
2 tablespoons of Virgin coconut oil
6-8 tablespoons of coconut flour (feel free to put more if you want it thicker)
20-24 ice cubes
2-4 tablespoons of protein powder (preferably from goat's milk)
2 teaspoons of pure vanilla extract
2 tablespoons of flax seeds ground

Directions:
1. First, you place the entire ingredients in a blender and process at high speed until well combined.

You may require more or less of ice, depending on how you could want your smoothie to be.

Coconut Tropical Bliss Smoothie

Tips:
When you want to serve, you may sprinkle with dried coconut or even add a slice of pineapple to the glass.

Ingredients:
Almond Milk:
3 cups of distilled water
1 cup of raw almonds
Mix INS:
Fresh pineapple
2 tablespoons of coconut oil
Frozen bananas
Coconut cream (concentrate to taste)

Directions:
1. First, you blend nut milk in a high-speed blender.

2. After which you add remaining ingredients and blend until thoroughly mixed.

3. Then you adjust ingredients to your desired taste and thickness.

Coco nutty Green Smoothie

Ingredients:
4 HUGE handfuls of spinach
½ teaspoon of cinnamon
2 tablespoons of coconut oil
4 bananas (frozen)
2 cups of milk (raw is best)
2 teaspoons of vanilla

Directions:
1. First, you add the entire ingredients into a blender.

2. After which you blend until mixed.

3. Then you serve in a tall glass.

Creamy Coconut Cinnamon Smoothie

Tips:
1. I suggest you use coconut milk or fresh raw milk for this recipe.

2. Feel free to add natural sweetener as well, such as banana or a fresh pineapple, which gives it a nice tropical twist!

Ingredients:
2 medium frozen banana
1 teaspoon of vanilla extract
2 teaspoons of virgin coconut oil
3 cups of milk
2 heaping teaspoons of coconut cream concentrate
Dashes of cinnamon

Directions:
1. First, you place milk, banana, coconut cream concentrate, vanilla and cinnamon in blender.

2. After which you blend on high for about 30 seconds or until ingredients are well combined.

3. Then you slowly drizzle the virgin coconut oil into the mixture.

BULLETPROOF DIET SMOOTHIE

Dark Chocolate Raspberry Custard Smoothie

Ingredients:
4 tablespoons of organic cocoa powder (or preferably more to taste)
4-8 soy-free pastured egg yolks
1 teaspoon of organic vanilla extract
2 frozen bananas, for additional creaminess (it is optional)
3 cups of raw milk, plain kefir (preferably homemade, or coconut milk)
4 tablespoons of virgin coconut oil, melted (or preferably more to taste)
2 tablespoons of raw honey
Dashes of real sea salt
3 cups of organic frozen raspberries

Directions:
1. First, you blend all but the frozen ingredients until smooth.

2. After which you add fruit and blend to desired consistency.

3. Then you adjust all ingredients to taste and enjoy!

Energy Berry Smoothie

Note:
Make sure that the berries & banana are frozen.

Ingredients:
1 banana
½ cup of orange juice
6 tablespoons of protein powder (it is optional)
6-8 ice cubes
2 cups of following berries, (or a mixture) blueberries, raspberries, strawberries or peaches
1 cup of rice, almond, coconut milk, hazelnut, or regular milk
1 cup of water
6-8 tablespoons virgin coconut oil, melted

Directions:
1. First, you place the entire ingredients into blender except oil and slowly pour oil in while blending.

2. Then beat all ingredients for 2 -3 minutes, or until well mixed and blended.

Fresh Fruity Smoothie with Coconut Oil

Tips:
If you do not like the taste of an avocado, try putting one in this mixture and I assure you that you will not know it is there.

Ingredients:
4 medium apples, with skin (remove core)
2 peaches (remove pit)
8 oz. cups of plain yogurt
2 avocados (it is optional)
2 cups of red grapes
2 pears (remove core)
2 cups of strawberries (remove stems)
2 cups of raw milk
4 tablespoons of virgin coconut oil

Directions:
1. First, you place the entire ingredients in a blender and blend until smooth.

2. After that, if you find the smoothie thick, I suggest you add more milk until it reaches your preferred consistency.

3. Finally, you place leftover smoothie in the refrigerator to enjoy later.

Fruit-Coconut Smoothie

Ingredients:
1 ¼ cups of organic vanilla yogurt
½ cup of frozen blueberries
½ cup of melted coconut oil
2 ripe bananas
½ cup of shredded coconut
2 tablespoons of whey protein

Directions:
1. First, you put everything except oil in the blender and blend until combined.

2. Then add the oil and process until well mixed.

Tips: If you want an even sweeter smoothie, I suggest you add 2 teaspoons of honey

Fruity Tropical Smoothie

Ingredients:
2 tablespoons of coconut flour
2 large organic bananas (peeled and mashed)
2 cups of fresh strawberries, sliced
20-24 ice cubes (it is optional)
6 tablespoons of virgin coconut oil (melted)
4 tablespoons of organic honey
2 cups of unsweetened pineapple chunks
4 organic kiwis (peeled and halved)
4 large organic mangoes (peeled and cubed)

Directions:
1. First, you combine virgin coconut oil, organic coconut flour, organic honey and mashed banana in small bowl.

2. After that, you mix well, incorporating oil thoroughly.

3. After which you pour into blender and add all other ingredients, except ice cubes.

4. At this point, you puree on high until well blended, and then blend for another 1 minute.

5. If mixture is too thick for your taste, I suggest you add some water, or add the ice and blend on high until ice crushed.

BULLETPROOF DIET SMOOTHIE

Get Your Greens Smoothie

Ingredients:
2 tablespoons of ground whole golden flax seed
2 scoops of Chocolate Goat Milk Protein
2 teaspoons of Virgin Coconut Oil, liquefied
2 large handful of whole spinach leaves
2 scoops of Mint Antioxidant Omega 3 Greens
3 - 4 cups of raw milk
2 frozen bananas (peeled and sliced into chunks)

Directions:
1. First, you combine the entire ingredients in a blender and then blend until smooth.

2. After that, you will find it thick, frothy & delicious!

Hot Cocoa

Ingredients:
2 tablespoons of Cocoa Powder
½ teaspoons of organic whole sugar (minimum)
2 tablespoons of Virgin Coconut Oil
Pinch of Himalayan salt

Directions:
1. First, you pour boiling water into a mug and let sit for about 20 seconds.

2. After which you empty the water and put one tablespoon full of the virgin coconut oil in it.

3. After that, it melts quickly as you stir in one tablespoonful of cocoa powder and a pinch of Himalayan salt.

4. At this point, you use a minimum of ½ teaspoon of whole organic sugar to cut the bitterness of the cocoa and then add stevia drops to taste. It is usually about 24 drops.

5. Then you pour boiling water in the cup, stir, and add cream or milk to taste.

6. Feel free to use other sweeteners can be used.

Iced Coconut Mocha Cappuccino

Ingredients:
1 cup of organic whole raw milk (or coconut milk)
2 tablespoons of coconut oil, melted (it is optional)
1 ¼ cups of cold, strong coffee (partly frozen if you wish)
4-8 ice cubes
4 tablespoons of fudge sauce, cold

Directions:
1. First, you place the entire ingredients except coconut oil in blender and blend until well combined, pouring coconut oil into the cappuccino a steady stream.

2. Then top with freshly whipped cream and enjoy!

Hot Fudge Sauce

Ingredients:
1 cup of cocoa powder
8 tablespoons of butter
3 teaspoons of vanilla extract
1 cup of sugar (plus 4 tablespoons)
1 ¼ cups of heavy cream
2-4 tablespoons of coconut oil

Directions:
1. First, you combine all ingredients except vanilla extract in a saucepan over medium heat.

2. Then when butter melts and is well mixed in, you turn heat up to high and bring fudge to a boil, whisking constantly.

3. After which you boil for 1 minute.

4. After that, you remove from heat and stir in vanilla.

5. Finally, you store in the refrigerator and do not eat it all at once.

Non-Dairy Coconut-Mocha Coffee Creamer

Ingredients:
2 cups of Coconut Cream Concentrate
4-6 tablespoons of organic cocoa powder
2 cups of Gold Label Virgin Coconut Oil
1 - 2 teaspoons of concentrated stevia powder or honey (or to taste)

Directions:
1. First, you gently soften or melt coconut oil and coconut cream until you can stir them.

2. After which you add sweetener and cocoa and mix until thoroughly combined.

3. Then you pour into small-lidded jars and refrigerate so it sets up properly without separating.

Directions to use:
1. You should mix one or more spoonsful into coffee or hot chocolate and then keeps well.

2. This recipe is great for traveling.

Pecan Coconut Chocolate Milk

Ingredients:
½ cup of pecans
6 tablespoons of virgin or expeller pressed coconut oil
2-4 tablespoons of raw honey
3 cups of organic whole milk
4 tablespoons of organic cocoa powder

Directions:
1. First, you add all ingredients except coconut oil to blender.

2. After which you blend until smooth and with the blender still running, slowly drizzle melted/cool coconut oil into mix.

3. Then you pour into a frosty mug or a large glass, fill with ice and serve.

4. Enjoy.

Carrot Coconut Candy

Ingredients:
2 cups of whole organic cane sugar
¼ teaspoon of salt
½ cup of coconut cream concentrates
2 pounds of grated carrots
½ cup of honey
2 cups of shredded coconut (divided use)
Juice and zest of four lemons

Directions:
1. First, you place the grated carrot, sugar, honey, and salt in a saucepan over medium high heat.

2. After which you stir until the sugar melts.

3. At this point, you add the lemon juice and zest, reduce heat, and simmer uncovered for about 30 minutes until carrots are tender and juice is syrupy.

4. After that, you let cool and then you transfer mixture to a food processor along with 1 cup of the shredded coconut and the coconut cream concentrate.

5. This is the point when you process until a thick paste forms.

6. In addition, you roll into truffle-sized balls and roll balls in the remaining shredded coconut.

7. Then you place on a lined baking sheet.

8. Finally, you let dry for a day on the baking sheet before placing in a covered container where they will keep up to 1 week.

Post-Holiday Power Smoothie

Tips:
This recipe is a yummy and nourishing powerhouse and it also perfect for breakfast or a pick me up that will have you back on track and going strong for hours.

Ingredients:
2-4 tablespoons of virgin coconut oil, melted
½ cup of organic rolled oats
2 teaspoons of vanilla
Dash salt
4 cups of frozen strawberries (or any frozen fruit of your choice)
3 cups of grass-fed milk, plain kefir (or coconut milk)
2 bananas, fresh or frozen
2 tablespoons of green food powder
2 tablespoons of raw honey
8 soy-free egg yolks (it is optional, but add lots of great nutrition and healthy fat for long lasting energy)

Directions:
First, you blend the entire ingredient except the fruit until mixed after which you add fruit and then blend until smooth.
Enjoy.

Quick Tropical Coconut Smoothie

Ingredients:
4-6 large bananas, fresh or frozen
4 cups of coconut milk
4 tablespoons of coconut oil (or coconut cream concentrate)
½ cup of flax seeds
4-8 cups of pineapple juice (or preferably raw pineapple and increased coconut milk)
8-12 cups of frozen mango chunks
4-6 cups of unpacked fresh spinach or a pinch of spirulina (it is optional)
4 tablespoons of hemp hearts (or hemp protein powder)
Raw honey or dates to sweeten (optional, and usually not needed)

Directions:
1. First, you add the entire ingredients, except for any frozen fruit in a high-powered, high capacity blender.

2. At this point, if you are opting for spinach and/or dates, this is the time to add it! I usually start out on the lower end of the liquids and increase as required.

3. After which you start blender out at low speed and slowly increase to high, allowing all of the flax seeds (and spinach) to liquefy.

4. After that, you should have a large amount of liquid yummiest! To this, you will add your frozen mangoes, until your reach required amount and consistency.

5. I suggest you add purer pineapple juice to get the desired tropical flavor, if it's lacking.

6. Enjoy!

Note: this smoothie is creamy, sweet, and delicious!

Raspberries & Cream Breakfast Smoothie

Tips:
This recipe is rich, creamy, fruity and very filling.

Ingredients:
1 ¼ cups of milk
1 teaspoon of vanilla extract (or vanilla powder)
6-8 tablespoons of rolled oats
2-4 tablespoons of coconut oil, melted
½ cup of heavy cream
2 cups of frozen raspberries
Dash ground nutmeg
2 honey date (it is optional)

Directions
1. First, you combine the entire ingredients except raspberries and coconut oil and let soak for about an hour or overnight.

2. After which you place the entire ingredients except coconut oil into a blender and blend until smooth while pouring coconut oil into blender in a steady stream.

3. Finally, you pour into a glass and enjoy!

Raspberry Coconut Smoothie

Ingredients:
2 grated apple
4 tablespoons of virgin coconut oil
4 cups of unsweetened coconut milk
16 ice cubes
2 frozen bananas
2 cups of frozen raspberries
4 tablespoons of chia seeds
½ cups of unsweetened organic shredded coconut

Directions:
1. First, you place all ingredients (except ice) in the blender.

2. After which you blend on high for about 1-2 minutes.

3. After that, you add in ice cubes, blend on 'frozen drinks' mode or use ice crusher to blend cubes.

4. Then you blend until smooth.

BULLETPROOF DIET SMOOTHIE

Raspberry Peach Melba Smoothie

Tip:
This recipe is perfect for a nutritious breakfast on the go and keeps you growing strong until lunch.

Ingredients:
4-8 organic eggs OR 2-4 tablespoons of goat milk protein powder
6 tablespoons of melted virgin coconut oil
2 teaspoons of vanilla extract
3 cups of plain kefir (preferably homemade)
2 tablespoons of raw honey
1 ¼ cups of frozen raspberries
1 ¼ cups of frozen peaches

Directions:
1. First, you add kefir, eggs or protein powder, honey and coconut oil, blend to mix before frozen ingredients.

2. Finally, you add frozen fruit and vanilla, blend until smooth.

3. Make sure you serve immediately.

Rise & Shine Breakfast Smoothie

Ingredients:
2 whole mangos, fresh or frozen
2 or 4 frozen bananas
2 tablespoons of freshly ground flax seed (it is optional)
4 tablespoons of coconut oil, melted (more/less as needed)
Coconut flakes
3 cups of kefir, yogurt or buttermilk
4 handfuls of strawberries, fresh or frozen
2-6 tablespoons of raw honey
Raw egg yolks (it is optional)

Directions:
1. First, you pour your choice of cultured dairy into the blender.

2. After which you add in mangos, strawberries, bananas and honey (add flax seed and/or egg yolks if you wish).

3. After that, you give it a whirl until smooth and while it is blending, you add coconut oil and let it run for a minute more.

4. Finally, you pour into a tall, large glass and top with coconut flakes and extra ground flax seeds if you wish.

Sensational Banana Strawberry Smoothie

Ingredients:
2-4 medium strawberries + one additional strawberry for decoration (it is optional)
2 tablespoons of coconut oil, melted
6 small frozen bananas
2 ½ cups of milk
2 raw egg yoke

Directions:
1. First, you chop bananas and strawberries and put them in the blender.

2. After which you pour the milk, and egg yolk in.

3. At this point, right before you start blending pour in the coconut oil.

4. After that, you blend until smooth.

5. Finally, you pour into a glass and garnish with the extra strawberry if you wish.

6. Enjoy!

Strawberries & Coconut Cream Protein Shake

Ingredients:
2 cups of frozen strawberries (or to taste)
2 scoops of vanilla ice cream or coconut ice cream (it is optional)
2-4 tablespoons of coconut oil, melted
2 cups of whole raw milk (or coconut milk)
1 teaspoon of vanilla extract or powder
2-4 scoops of protein powder

Directions:
1. First, you place all ingredients except coconut oil into a blender and blend until smooth.

2. After which you pour coconut oil into blender in a steady stream while blending.

3. Finally, you pour into a tall glass.

4. Enjoy!

BULLETPROOF DIET SMOOTHIE

Strawberry Coconut Bliss Smoothie

Ingredients:
2-6 soy-free organic eggs
2-6 tablespoons of virgin coconut oil, melted
3-4 cups of organic frozen strawberries
3 cups of plain kefir (preferably homemade)
2 tablespoons of honey
¼ teaspoon of organic cinnamon
½ teaspoon of organic natural vanilla

Directions:
1. First, you add kefir, you needed amount of eggs, coconut oil and honey to the blender and combine thoroughly.

2. Remember, that the extra eggs and coconut oil provide even long lasting satisfaction and energy.

3. After that, you add vanilla, cinnamon and strawberries.

4. After which you adjust amount according to required thickness and blend on medium, then high speed until thoroughly combined, thick and creamy.

5. Then you garnish with additional strawberries and a sprinkle of cinnamon if you wished.

6. Serve immediately.

Strawberry Lemon Coconut Smoothie

Ingredients:
2-6 soy-free organic eggs
2-6 tablespoons of coconut oil (melted)
1 teaspoon of organic pure vanilla extract
Dashes of salt
3 cups of organic raw milk (plain kefir or milk of choice)
2 tablespoons of raw honey
2-4 cups of organic frozen strawberries (it all depends on your desired consistency)
½ teaspoon of organic lemon oil flavoring

Directions:
1. First, you put the organic raw milk, organic eggs, raw honey and coconut oil in a blender and blend thoroughly.

2. After which you add the remaining ingredients and blend until smooth. \

3. Serve immediately.

Strawberry Mango Coconut Delight

Ingredients:
8 pastured soy-free egg yolks
2 tablespoons of honey
2 cups of frozen mangos
Dashes of sea salt
3 cups of raw milk (kefir or coconut milk)
2-4 tablespoons of virgin coconut oil, melted
2 cups of frozen strawberries
2 teaspoons of vanilla extract

Directions:
1. First, you put the raw milk, egg yolks, virgin coconut oil, honey in a blender and blend until smooth.

2. After which you add remaining ingredients and blend until it reached your desired consistency.

3. Finally, you serve with additional fruit if you wish.

4. Enjoy!

Strawberry Vanilla Coconut Smoothie

Ingredients:
1 ¼ cups of coconut or organic whole raw milk
2-4 tablespoons of coconut oil, melted
1 cup of plain organic yogurt (preferably Greek or goat's milk is best!)
3 teaspoons of vanilla extract
16 large strawberries, fresh or frozen (if you using fresh add ice cubes to taste)

Directions:
1. First, you blend everything except coconut oil.

2. After which you slowly pour coconut oil in while blender is running.

3. At this point, you pour into a glass, garnish with some dried coconut or a fresh strawberry if you wish.

4. Enjoy!

Tropical Cocktail

Ingredients:
3 tablespoons of coconut concentrate
2 ripe bananas
2 teaspoons of lime juice
4 tablespoons of coconut oil, liquefied
300 ml water
1 cup of frozen mango
240 ml orange juice
6 tablespoons of vanilla yogurt

Ingredients:
1. First, you mix water and coconut cream concentrate together until well blended.

2. After which you put everything except oil in a blender and process until you get a smooth texture of a drink.

3. After that, you add oil and process again.

4. Feel free to add 3 drops of stevia to give sweeter taste.

Note: this recipe is good for a hot sunny day!

CILANTRO WITH SPINACH SMOOTHIE

Ingredients:
9 ice cube
4 ½ bananas
2 ½ of fresh spinach
½-inch fresh ginger
1 ½ peeled lime
1 cup of fresh cilantro

Directions:
1. First, you pour the cilantro, spinach and ice in the blender.
2. After which you blend on a high speed for a few seconds.
3. Then you add banana, ginger and lime and blend until it is smooth.

KIWI AND APPLE GREEN SMOOTHIE

Ingredients:
2 chopped apples
Water
4 skinned kiwis
2 packed cups of spinach
Sprinkle of cinnamon (optional)

Directions:
1. First, you pour the entire ingredient in the blender and blend until well incorporated.

2. Make sure you serve immediately.

COCONUT, APPLE AND YOGURT GREEN SMOOTHIE

Ingredients:
2 peeled and chopped apple
4 tablespoons of shaved fresh coconut
2-cups of ice
2 chopped and frozen bananas
1-cup of plain Greek yogurt (low fat)
1 cup of coconut milk
2 cups of spinach

Directions:
1. First, you pour the entire ingredient in the blender and blend until very smooth.
2. Make sure you serve immediately.

CHOCOLATE COVERED CHERRY GREEN SMOOTHIES

Ingredients:
2 teaspoons cinnamon
Four bananas
4 cups unsweetened almond milk
4 cups fresh spinach
6-tablespoons cacao powder
4 cups cherries (pitted)

Direction:
1. First, you place the spinach and almond milk in the blender.
2. After which you blend until smooth.
3. Then you add the remaining fruits and blend them together.

RAW CHOCOLATE ALMOND GREEN SMOOTHIE

Ingredients:
2 bananas
2 tablespoons of ground flax seed
½ the water of a young coconut
1-cup raw organic almond milk
1 cup of filtered water
½ teaspoon of vanilla
2 cups of ice or to taste
4 tablespoons of raw organic cacao
2 tablespoons of raw organic almond butter
Pinch of salt
½ the meat of a young coconut
2 cups of fresh spinach
One pitted date

Directions:
1. First, you pour the entire ingredient in the blender (excluding the ice).
2. After which you blend for a few seconds.
3. Then you add the ice and blend until smooth.

AVOCADO GREEN SMOOTHIE

Ingredients:
2 apples
1 avocado
1 ½ cups of water
2 stock of celery
2 bananas
3 cups fresh baby spinach

Tip: if you want the green smoothie recipe to be sweeter, you add a natural sweetener, like agave, nectar, to taste.

Directions:
1. First, you put the entire ingredient in the blender (one at a time).
2. Then you blend until it is smooth.

BULLETPROOF DIET SMOOTHIE

DATES AND CASHEWS GREEN SMOOTHIE

Ingredients:
2-tablespoons of ground flaxseed
Six pitted dates
1-teaspoon vanilla
½ cup of roasted cashews
4 cups vanilla almond milk (unsweetened)
2 frozen bananas
6 cups baby spinach

Tip:
It is high in calories, but rich in its nutritional content.

Direction:
1. First, you pour the entire ingredient in a blender.
2. After which you blend until it is smooth.

CONCLUSION
Thanks for reading through this book; if you follow judiciously the recipes outlined above, you will sleep better, feel better, think better, have more energy and loss weight without effort.

Remember, the only bad action you can take is no action at all.

www.ingramcontent.com/pod-product-compliance
Lightning Source LLC
Chambersburg PA
CBHW080022130526
44591CB00036B/2578